Let's Chat: How Conversation Increases Sales

Written by Linda Pike
With Deborah Littleton

i

Let's Chat: How Conversation Increases Sales

Citations:

B.J. Gallagher, Mac Anderson, "Trouble Tree," *Learning to Dance in the Rain: The Power of Gratitude* (Illinois: Simple Truths, LLC, 2009)
Juliette Gordon Low, "Make New Friends," *Girl Scout Song Book;* words only (Girl Scouts, Inc., 1925)
qualify. Dictionary.com. *Dictionary.com Unabridged*. Random House, Inc.
http://dictionary.reference.com/browse/qualify (accessed: February 24, 2015)
Raymond Douglas Stanford and Bob Proctor, quotes used by permission (Arizona: Proctor Gallagher Institute, 2015)
 "Yada yada yada." Used by permission from Castlerock Entertainment

ISBN: 1517562279
ISBN-13: 978-1517562274

Acknowledgements

Special Thanks: I'd really like to thank my Mom. Although she passed away in 2010, I think of her every day. The reason I could write this book was the confidence she instilled in me at a very young age. She inspired me to always try something new, no matter what the outcome may be, and luckily most of my choices turned out to be the right ones! Thank you to my awesome husband who constantly tells me, "Stay true to yourself," and my wonderful children who inspire me every day.

A huge shout-out to my niece Deanna for coming up with the name of the book. Since it was my first book, I wanted to wait until I knew what I wanted to say, before even thinking of the title. Then it was just obvious when it became all about communication, and Deanna struck just the right note, providing the perfect title. I'd really like to thank all of those students that ran up to me over the years, asking for my book(s). They really encouraged me to write this first book. Thank you Deborah, it's been a long run and we did it!!

Let's Chat: How Conversation Increases Sales

Table of Contents

Intro

Another book about selling? Yes! I wrote this book with the intention of sharing my passion of the greatest job—sales! Helping your customer decide the best product or service for them is so gratifying and rewarding. As you read the last page, I hope you have gained the confidence you may have lacked on page one and have become as passionate as I am!

This is the basis of the book. With the state of the economy, it's really humbled us all. We really need to take a step back and look at how we're acting: The good, the bad, and the ugly. Why do customers buy from certain salespeople versus others? What do they say differently that other salespeople don't say?

I really, truly believe it's that these successful salespeople are honestly just being themselves. They are authentic. Most especially, they're passionate about what they're selling, and they really care about helping people. It really doesn't matter what you're selling, but it matters that you're passionate and just chatting with the customer, asking the right qualifying questions.

If you're passionate about anything, you're going to make it happen. You will succeed because you're passionate about your product and helping your customers. Notice I said customers. There will be a lot of them if you do it right, even in this millennial economic downturn.

We have all had to change in these economic times. Salespeople used to be greedier and cockier—resting on the laurels of their selling past. They've had to step back and analyze why that's not working for them now. The laws of supply and demand are taking a stronghold on sales, as there are now more salespeople than customers. And times are going to be really lean if you are not true to yourself. Customers won't be buying from you. They'll go onto the more authentic salesperson.

We all need to take a long, hard look in the mirror and regroup. We really need to get back to the basics of sales, following the right process without skipping steps. And it's really important that you simply be yourself, no matter what you're selling.

Jobs are much harder to come by, startups are fizzle-outs because they don't have enough time to catch the flame of entrepreneurship—as their salespeople jump to the next floating ship. Everyone has to humble themselves and may have to drop down a step or two.

I really feel that if we could all have somebody else's job for a day, how much better it would be. Humankind would be improved. People would have a better understanding of what everyone does, and they would be more understanding. So take a step back—humble yourself. It's a sign of the times.

Another reason I decided to write this book is because my passion is to help people succeed. At every seminar that I do on sales training, people run up to me afterward asking, "Do you have a book?" So I decided to write a book. When I met Deborah Littleton, as I was flying to my seminar in Sacramento, she renewed the sense of urgency.

I'd been putting it together, in my head, and she encouraged me to just start writing. We were emailing back and forth for about a year when I realized that I was just so busy, that it made sense to collaborate.

I've been training retail salespeople for twenty years, and one of the neatest parts about training is the feedback. It is the coolest thing when you have training classes and people want to learn how to sell. I get so excited when I get emails and phone calls from past students and they say they were number one in the first month—they sold 150 percent of their goal. It's just amazing. That's the essence of why I'm writing this book.

I want to share with all of you who are reading this book the rewards and the gratification. That really validates why I am a trainer. I love to help people succeed. My passion is to help people to be better salespeople.

I can't say enough about customer service. It really starts with a simple smile. If I have to repeat this forty-seven thousand times in this book, I will. You know, people come to work mad. People come to work sad. People come to work angry. And for those people who come to work happy, they're going to sell more because they're going to portray that in their nonverbal communication with a simple smile.

So please keep this in mind, throughout the book, while you're reading. I wrote this—for the simple reason—to help you to become better at selling, by simply communicating with your customer.

When you think about it, it all started when you were in a high chair, trying to sell yourself, or sell something. I know you're not going to remember it, but you either yelled or reached out to your mom's arms. And when you got bigger, you attempted many times to have that piece of candy.

"Mom can I have that piece of candy?" And the reply was always, "No. Not now." Or she might have said, "After lunch." So you'd try again. "Can I have that candy? Please can I have that piece of candy?" And you got that same reply. But maybe after that third or fourth time, when you asked for the piece of candy, your mom said, "Oh, here. Have it."

Well guess what? You just sold yourself. So for those that think they can't sell anything, think about it in a new light. You started selling yourself, almost from day one. Crying to get fed. Crying to get changed. So in essence, it's really that you're selling yourself.

I don't want this to be a typical sales book: How do you sell? There are thousands of those books out there. I want everyone reading this book to get a clearer understanding of what it takes to become a successful salesperson. I think the very first thing on the list is confidence.

Chapter 1: Confidence

One important key to success is self-confidence. An important key to self-confidence is preparation.
—Arthur Ashe

If you want to achieve widespread impact and lasting value, be bold.
—Howard Schultz

If you can imagine it, you can achieve it. If you can dream it, you can become it.
—William Arthur Ward

It's not what you are that holds you back, it's what you think you're not.
—Denis Waitley

If you don't have confidence in yourself, how can you expect to sell something? Remember what I said before? The first thing you sell is yourself. Remember in your high chair? Remember when you were growing up and you wanted that candy bar? That's what it takes—confidence.

How many people have you met in your life have said the following? "Wow! I can't believe that you just sold that!" or "I can't believe how easily you can sell. Wow!" And they wish they could be a salesperson. They wish they could be like you. They really could be like you.

Or maybe you're the one who wishes you could be like that salesperson. As you know, those are just excuses—and we have a whole chapter dedicated to excuses later in the book. So let's work on your confidence. How can you become confident?

Step number one is saying, "I can. I can. I can." You must say this instead of "I can't. I can't. I can't." It's really elementary— like selling yourself for that candy bar. Just like *The Little Train That Could* saying, "I think I can. I think I can. I know I can. I know I can." I know you may think, "How silly is that?!" But it's true.

I remember my very first seminar. I'll admit I didn't sleep the night before. I had everything down pat, but I was really nervous. If I told you anything different, it wouldn't be the truth. I was scared to speak in front of a crowd.

I got up in the morning and went about my morning routine. I made sure that I had a great breakfast. I went over my notes, went over my agenda. I got in my car and went to the store, to do the seminar. I parked the car. I have to tell you, my knees were shaking. But I kept saying to myself over and over, "I can. I can. I can. I will. I will. I will."

The law of three has power, just like in good comedy. Comedians get the deepest and longest laughs on that repetition. If you tell yourself "I can. I can. I can," you're much more likely to intrinsically believe it.

I remember when I was young and my mom made me take dance class. And along came the end of the year recital. I didn't want to do it, but she made me do the recital. At the end of the recital, I said to my mom, "If you make me do this again, I'll cry forever." She just looked at me and said, "You did a great job." That's how nervous I was, but guess what? I did it!

So getting back to that parking lot—before my first training seminar—and I'm sitting in the car. And now I'm watching people arrive at my seminar. People that I don't know. People who want to be there. People who might not want to be there. Executives. Salespeople. Managers. Maybe even their trainers. It was all a little overwhelming.

I watched them all enter the building, and I finally got the courage to get out of the car. I entered the building and went to the room to do the seminar. I introduced myself, "Hi. I'm Linda Pike, and I'm here to do the sales training seminar."

I had a very warm welcome. Maybe they couldn't tell that I was nervous. But I will tell you, I was very nervous. You would have thought I was going onstage and had stage fright! A lot of this was just anxiety because I was going to be speaking in public, but I knew my topic thoroughly, so I was halfway there. But have I said it enough? I was still nervous.

So they took me to the podium. I got all set up and just started introducing myself to everyone. I said "Hi. Good morning. My name is Linda Pike. It's so nice to meet you. Thank you for coming." I have to say I felt a lot more at ease. It helped with the nerves, to break the ice.

When I started the seminar, I introduced myself. I told them where I was from, where I live, how many kids I had. Then I explained to them that that the sole reason I was there was that I just wanted to help them to be successful at their jobs.

At the end of the day, people were asking me how I had so much energy so early in the morning, and I told them "I love what

I do. I love helping people succeed, and I hope you learned something today."

One thing that helped get me through it was just to get up there and do it. It was something I learned from my mother and the dance class, but sometimes it takes reminding. And to be honest, thinking about it now, in public speaking you're really just selling yourself—wanting people to listen—on a larger scale. The more prepared you are, just like I was that first morning, the less there is to stress about.

What I really think eased my mind even more was that people were feeling that I'm really down to earth. I've never been on a power trip. And just by the way I was introducing myself, they started becoming more comfortable with me, so I was more comfortable with them. They saw my passion and energy in wanting to help them be successful, and that just set the tone for the seminar.

I will never forget, many years down the road, this one lady raised her hand at the beginning of the seminar. She said, "I don't want to be here. I don't know why I'm here. I was forced to come here." I said to her, "I appreciate you coming. I hope that you will stay for the entire seminar, and I hope that you will learn something." I thanked her for coming.

Two-thirds of the way into the seminar, she raised her hand again. This was the first time I'd heard anything from her since earlier that day, when she'd complained about being there. When I called on her, she said, "I want to apologize to you, Linda."

I asked her why, and she said, "Because this is the best seminar I've ever been to. I've learned more about myself and more about how to sell than in my entire lifetime." This lady was in her late forties or early fifties. As you can imagine, that just made my day.

So let's get back to confidence. How can you get confidence to be a better salesperson? We all have insecurities. If someone tells you they don't have insecurities, they're not being truthful. As soon as you realize that everybody has insecurities, it will make you feel more confident. It sounds funny, but it's true. It really is.

Remember how nervous and scared I was before I walked into that building for the first seminar that I did? It's okay to have insecurities. I will teach you how to overcome them.

I have a great confidence story to share with you. I had a student in a sales class that I was teaching. I'll call her Sandra. And the first day of class she said to me, "Linda, I have to tell you that I almost didn't make it today." I asked Sandra why, and she answered, "Because I have no confidence in myself, that I can learn how to sell." I said to her, "That's absolutely silly, and from this moment forward, I don't want you thinking that. "

Sandra actually started crying. And I said, "You have nothing to cry about. Today is the first day that you will be learning how to sell."

It's really amazing to me that we have such a lack of confidence in ourselves that prevents us from becoming more successful. So in this book I hope to help encourage you, as you're reading, to gain confidence. There are so many sales books that say, over and over again: Don't be afraid. You create your own fear. You're scared. Whatever. And while that's really true, the bottom line is that if you don't have confidence in yourself, then you're not going to be as successful as you could be.

It was amazing when that student, Sandra, came to me. She talked to me for a while. I told her, "Today is the first day of class, and I guarantee you, at the end of this class, you will have confidence in yourself." And watching her through the five-day class, I could see that Sandra was listening because I also teach a listening skills class. I kept looking at her and she was just listening, and soaking it all in, because she really wanted to learn. Sandra's just one of the amazing stories that I can't wait to share as you read on in this book.

Again, I cannot stress enough the importance of confidence. Once you learn to be confident, you can do anything you set out to do. I'm hesitant in even continuing right now, because I want you to put the book down. Sit back and think about it: Confidence is really a key factor in anything that you do in sales, creating sales, closing deals, goals for growth, etc.

The fact is that you really need to look in the mirror. Do you like what you see? When you wake up in the morning, do you have a positive attitude? You've got to be confident. If you're not confident, then you won't be successful. It's really as simple as that. I don't mean to be so direct, but how else can you be when you want to stress a point?

I've been told I'm a "Tell-it-like-it-is-window-person." That's what I do. I tell it like it is. Why beat around the bush? Let's take my student Sandra for instance, who said she didn't have confidence. And I said that by the end of the class she would be confident. Sandra was, and now she's the top salesperson in her region—all because she's confident.

That's all you need: Confidence in yourself—that you can sell anything—and you will be successful!

Chapter 2: Passion

There is no passion to be found
playing small in settling for a life that
is less than the one you are capable of
living.—Nelson Mandela

Passion persuades.—Anita Roddick

You've got to have **_passion!!!_** I have to bold, underline *and* italicize this word because you need to know exactly how important it is! I just know I'll end up being the P.S. Person (Passionate Salesperson) off of this first book because I'm passionate about sharing that lesson!

If you are passionate about anything, you will be able to sell it. Basically with sales, if you can sell yourself, you can sell anything. I've talked about it already, but if you love what you sell and you're passionate about that product, then you're going to sell it! You will be successful.

I recall that one of my sons was at work one day. He is an outside salesperson and got a call from a company that does business with his current employer. My son has a very good job, but this other company was very impressed with him. They wanted him to apply as they were very interested in hiring him.

My son called me, and we talked about it. He told me, "You know, I appreciate them calling, but I don't like the product that they sell." We talked about it a little bit further, about the product, and why he didn't like it. My son told me, "I can't sell something or work for a company if I don't like the product." I have to say, even though I am his mom, that's great integrity.

It's true. You can't sell something well if you don't like what you're selling. Your customers will perceive that. So before you start a job—before you say, "Yes, I'll take this job"—make sure you love the product that they sell!

I even talk passionately when I bring up passion because that's how I've sold myself. People all over the United States have told me, after going to my sales seminars, *"Linda!* You are the most passionate person I've ever met." And I always answer, "I *love* helping people *succeed.* That is my passion, to help people succeed."

Just as I'd said in the intro, that's why I'm writing this book, because if you can take anything away from this book, then you'll be a better salesperson. And I know there are so many sales books out there, but are they passionate about teaching selling? Are they passionate about teaching good selling techniques? It's so key, to be passionate about what you do.

I'm not talking about being so over the top that nobody can stand being around you as a salesperson. I'm talking about being really, truly passionate about the product that you sell. I used to tell people "I *love* my job! I love *selling* this!" And the reaction on people's faces was amazement, and they always said, "Wow! We can tell!"

In order to get passionate, you have to realize that you're born with passion. You just have to tap into it and use it. A lot of people are afraid to show their feelings of passion for fear that people will think they're crazy—that they're over the top. But again, it's the way that you portray yourself. It's all in your approach.

You have to have some kind of passion for what you're selling in order to sell it. If you're just operating by rote and not feeling it—or just speaking in monotone—you're just an everyday salesperson. But if you show some passion in your selling process, you're going to be the standout—the one that people will want to buy from.

Deborah shared that actors who excel have to be passionate about their part—and fully believe in it—to be believable. The more they immerse themselves in the script which is their product, and memorize it, the more we catch the passion in their performance. It's sometimes palpable. That's what a customer needs to see in your passion, that your love of the product is right there on the surface.

Always keep in mind that if you don't make the sale, somebody else will. So why not be a little passionate about your product? I profess through the whole book that you need to be yourself. And your knowledge of your product is an extension of yourself, in sharing that information with your customer.

We all know that the selling process is like using a script. You need to know what to say and when to say it to a prospective customer in relation to their questions. If you're confident, you're passionate and you love your product, you will definitely sell the product.

So why are so many people awful at selling? It's because they lack the confidence, and they are not passionate. People can see right through the salesperson, and customers don't care whether the salesperson makes the sale or not. So it sets me apart from the competition. And it should now set you apart from your competition in making the sale.

Think back to things that you've bought in your lifetime and things that you've sold in your lifetime. How many really passionate salespeople are out there? Maybe you've had to buy things that were a necessity, and when you left the store you said, "Wow! If I didn't really need that, I really wouldn't have bought it from them. That salesperson was horrible!" Or maybe it was, "I'm never going back there again because they have terrible customer service!"

In my selling seminars I ask people, "Can you count on one hand the last time you got really good customer service?" And they sit back or rest their head on the chair, and they really can't think of anything. It's so easy to be nice, so why do people make it so difficult?

You also want to make sure that you never bring your problems to work. This keeps you from being as passionate about your product as you could be. There's a really good analogy on bringing your problems in, like a chip on your shoulder. It's a really good way of thinking about leaving your troubles on your doorstep:

A Story with Wisdom: The Trouble Tree
by Author Unknown

The carpenter I hired to help me restore an old farm house had just finished a rough first day on the job. A flat tire had caused him to miss an hour of work, his electric saw quit, and now his ancient pickup truck refused to start.

As I drove him home, he sat in stony silence. When we arrived he invited me in to meet his family. As we walked to the front door, he paused briefly at a small tree, touching the tips of the branches with both hands. When opening the door he underwent an amazing transformation. His tanned face was wreathed in smiles; he hugged his two small children and gave his wife a kiss.

Afterward he walked me to the car. We passed by the tree and my curiosity got the better of me.

I asked him about what I had seen him do earlier.

"Oh, that's my trouble tree," he replied. "I know I can't help having troubles on the job, but one thing's for sure, they don't belong in the house with my wife and children. So, I just hang them on the tree when I come home in the evening and then I just pick them up again in the morning.

"Funny thing, though," he smiled, "when I come out in the morning to pick 'em up, there ain't nearly as many as I remembered hanging there the night before."

You absolutely cannot bring your personal problems into the job and expect to be passionate about anything. If you're weighted down, you have to get it off your shoulder and breathe deeply on the way in through the door. The customer doesn't care about the night you had. Put your problems on your own trouble tree—even if it's just a trouble bush outside of your store!

There's also no room for ego with customers. If your customer feels squeezed out by your ego, they will leave your store. What I say in my training classes is, "If you have ego problems, check your ego at the door!"

If you're learning about selling a new product, you really need to stay true to yourself, and be yourself. Selling doesn't have to be that hard. It should be synonymous with relaxing.

Now persistence on your part? Yes! Hard work on your part? Definitely! But selling is the most gratifying job in my eyes. And it should be gratifying in your eyes, too, or you wouldn't have bought this book.

Being passionate isn't something that you can just turn on or practice. It's something that's a feeling inside. You have to feel free to show that side of you. You have your own personality. You can tell when someone is passionate or not, about their product, just by their feelings. You can also tell when someone doesn't care.

I don't want you to think that you can't get there if you're not quite feeling it. Some of us are more passionate than others. Keep in mind people can sense if you're passionate about helping them find the right product or service to buy.

You don't have to do cartwheels. What you do need to do is ask the right questions, listen to their answers and guide them to the right decision to make. It's amazing to think that your passion can help them buy something, which can be felt by your customer immediately with a simple smile!

When you aren't in tune with letting the passion come to the surface, you can try it on for size at home. You can practice your smile in the mirror, but let them be genuine. A mirror would be a great tool in your employee lounge—to check your attitude and practice your *real* smile prior to hitting the sales floor. You can even go so far as to videotape yourself for sales technique correction. Really, though, you ultimately want to sound genuine and not forced.

You can ask a friend, do I sound passionate about my product? You ask your customers, "Can you tell I'm excited about this product?" You can also tell the customer, "I'm very passionate about this!" Make sure to promote the name of the product in these professions, as it drives the point home and lets them know you're authentic.

I can't say it enough though, you really don't want to be over the top. There really is such a thing as too much, and you can drive a customer away with that tactic. It starts sounding desperate and forced. Stay authentic.

You can tell by my voice, I'm very passionate about helping people. Instead of saying, "I'm very passionate about helping people," I actually italicize it with my voice even when reading it out loud. Remember how I italicized **passion** at the beginning of this chapter? You can do that, too. You can share that passion. Italicizing with your voice is a technique, but the passion has to be a real feeling behind your voice.

See how you look to other people and practice sprinkling a liberal dose of passion into your selling process, talking about your product. Again, passion isn't something you can really practice as it comes from within, but the skills can help you get there. And just like that phrase, "Action leads to emotion," or "Fake it till you make it," if you're working on your delivery and still being yourself, you can be passionate about your product, too.

It's actually very cool when your customer tells you, "You know, I had no idea I was going to buy today. I had no intentions of buying today, but I did because you are so passionate about the product. It's *gotta* be good!" There's *no* better feeling than that.

Chapter 3: Staying True To Yourself

Dare to be yourself. —André Gide

Try not to become a man of success but a man of value.—Albert Einstein

Perfection of character is this: To live each day as if it were your last, without frenzy, without apathy, without pretense.—Marcus Aurelius

Always keep in mind—if you stay true to yourself, and always be yourself, then you will be very successful at sales. This is one of the real reasons for my writing this book.

So many people we deal with are on a power trip or have insecurities. If they just react to people as themselves, and who they are, they're much more likely to make the sale. We have all dealt with arrogant people, impatient people, very shy people, etc., both as customers and coworkers. We are so quick to judge someone before we get to know them.

Working in the retail industry, customers so often walk through the door—possibly with a bad experience in another retail establishment. These customers might come in with a chip on their shoulder but end up being the best people in the world because they found a new authentic salesperson. Those salespeople were most likely true to themselves, and acting like themselves, which means they're true to the customer.

In my thirty years of selling, I've worked with so many different types of people. I've had numerous people who I have worked for or who have worked for me. They tell me what they love so much about me is that I'm true to myself and I'm always myself.

Think about it, as you're sitting there reading this book. Get to know yourself. If you're shy, then you know that you have to acclimate yourself to being a salesperson. The passion may take a little more time in developing when you're shy, but you can do it! Remember what I said in the beginning of the book? I can. I can. I can…be passionate!

Selling is basically your stage, and you have to be true to yourself, so you might have to be a little more assertive than you already are by nature. But no matter what the arena—retail, outside sales or inside sales—people can tell right away if you're on a power trip.

I have a story to share about waiting on a customer once. Price didn't even come up. I explained the value of the product. She said to me midstream through the sale, "I am so enjoying this experience." I asked her, "What do you mean?"

She said, "The store that I was in before, the salesperson was just nasty, and arrogant, and could care less. But you care about what I'm buying. You care about who I am. You care about who it's for. I'm going to buy this regardless of anything else. It's been a pleasant experience." And she bought the product.

It's just who I am. It's who you need to be. Throughout this book, you're going to hear, "Be true to yourself, and always be yourself." And that doesn't mean when you feel like you're "onstage" to make that sale, you're still not true to yourself. It has to be you—wonderful you!

I remember one time watching a show with my grandson. It was all about being true to yourself. It's amazing. If you stay true to yourself, ultimately people will understand you and like you for being authentic. People will be able to tell you're a genuine, down-to-earth person.

It's not about winning a popularity contest. If you're an angry person, don't get into sales. You might want to stay in a cubicle. If you love interacting with, and helping people, this is the right book for you to read.

In thinking back on popularity—there are many who go from being a "nobody" in high school to becoming more assertive when they break away from the mold of how others perceived them. In fact, Deborah maintains that she became more outgoing by getting involved in theatre. She says that she found her voice there.

Sometimes it's a fresh start, away from the old crowd. And someone who was formerly on the shy side might come into their own when they start making some income from selling. It's always fun to go back to a high school reunion with a successful career under your belt. If that sounds like you or what you think you're capable of, keep reading!

If you're stuck in a rut, think of the last time that you didn't make the sale or you felt like you blew it. And you said, "Man, if I acted differently or if I said something different, then I probably would have made the sale." Or maybe you over-analyzed the way you conducted yourself. If you are true to yourself and are yourself every time, you will ultimately make more sales. Take my advice. It's true!

Selling can be so much fun if you enjoy it. You don't want to wake up in the morning and set yourself up for rejections to get you through the day. If you do, you're not going to have a very successful day.

Unfortunately in this profession, you do face more rejection on a daily basis. You need to learn how to deal with the rejection as it's really not personal. Rejection isn't bad. It happens. We cannot let it wreck our day. Shake it off ASAP. Ask yourself what good it does to hold onto that rejection.

Everyone deals with rejection in his or her own way. All I'm saying is that you need to shrug it off so it doesn't ruin your day. I look at it as an opportunity to regroup, think about what I said, what I didn't say, and move on!

Why am I a successful salesperson? I make sure that I sell the value. You could have ten people walk into your store. All of them want to buy a TV and all of them have their own thoughts on what kind of TV they want.

A TV is a TV right? Nope. Some people buy a particular brand and some buy for the size. Here's what you need to clarify: What is truly important to them about that TV. You do that by asking questions, listening to their answers, and finding out what is important to them.

In most cases when you do that, cost won't matter. Ask yourself how many purchases you made, spending more money than you anticipated because you had the right salesperson asking you the right questions, qualifying your needs, and you were really thankful for the help.

That doesn't mean being over the top. Have you ever met that salesperson that's so uppity that it's like they have to take a chill pill? Have you ever met the salesperson that says, "Yeah, I'm serious! Serious as a heart attack"? Anytime any salesperson says that to me, I say, "Oh, please don't have one. I really don't want you to be that serious."

Are they true to themselves? No. It's just a game to them. But if you're passionate about what you do—if you love what you sell and you show them the value—people are going to ask you if they can buy your product. People are going to ask, "Where do I sign?" Keep reading on.

Just as a side note, I was watching a news show and they were interviewing a Tony award winning actress who has also acted on TV. The newscaster was asking her how she became a singer. She actually said that when she was in high school, kids called her a bit of a dork. She liked to listen to out-of-the-ordinary music like Judy Garland and opera singers.

What she said that caught my attention was that she has always stayed true to herself and hasn't tried to act like anyone else. I thought that was an important thing to share. She was successful just by being herself. Endeavor to be true to yourself, and success will follow.

Chapter 4: Sincerity/Authenticity

Always do right. This will gratify
some people, and astonish the rest.
—Mark Twain

Let us remember that, as much has
been given us, much will be expected
from us, and that true homage comes
from the heart as well as from the
lips, and shows itself in deeds.
—Theodore Roosevelt

A great life is born in the soul, grown
in the mind, and lived from the
heart.—Suzanne Zoglio

It's absolutely mind boggling to me. People make things out to be more difficult than they are. If you really are staying true to yourself—meaning sincere and authentic—then customers don't see you as fake. The worst thing you can possibly do is to be fake and insincere.

This is all so important that it takes two chapters to impress on you. You won't sell anything if they can see that you're insincere. If the customer can relate to you as being real and caring about their needs, you are bound to make a sale. First the customer buys you! Second, if they see the value, they'll buy the service or product.

Deborah said that it's similar with actors. They are playing a part, but if they're not believable, nobody would watch them. The best actors are those that are authentically feeling real emotions versus being caught acting. If they just went through the motions and weren't believable, again, you wouldn't "buy" their performance.

Think about when you are a customer yourself, when you walk in and you really need help with an item or items that you want to purchase. It's bad if that salesperson comes across as being in a bad mood or that they're fake and insincere. The tone is set and you're not comfortable with that salesperson. You have lost your trust in your salesperson. You'll be giving them the buying signals, which we'll go into more detail about in the sales process.

People don't think about others' feelings often enough. You have to understand one very important aspect of this whole thing is that you're not going to make the sale unless you follow all the steps and you understand the process. And if you hit all the steps—along with being sincere—you're going to make the sale.

Customers can really sense when you are faking it or that you don't care. For example, if a customer walks in and you're on the phone and don't acknowledge their presence or you realize right off the bat that they're not going to be buying from you and you don't address them properly—they will know. You will not sell anything. You will just be creating your own poor reality. Don't ever go there.

You cannot assume anything or you cement your inability to make the sale. If you're assuming they're not there to buy, it's your new reality. You must connect in a sincere way with the customer. Anything less can mean that they won't want to connect with you, and you won't get the sale.

I can't say it enough: Assuming anything will be an automatic disconnect maneuver, and they will look for a different salesperson or even leave your store. So be authentic and open to success.

Remember: Sincerity leads to success. Do your best to stay real, and you will definitely make more sales.

Chapter 5: Rapport

*Each morning when I open my eyes I
say to myself: I, not events, have the
power to make me happy or unhappy
today. I can choose which it shall be.
Yesterday is dead, tomorrow hasn't
arrived yet. I have just one day, today,
and I'm going to be happy in it.*
—Groucho Marx

*Good humor is a tonic for mind and
body. It is the best antidote for
anxiety and depression. It is a
business asset. It attracts and keeps
friends. It lightens human burdens. It
is the direct route to serenity and
contentment.—Grenville Kleiser*

Work is love made visible.
—Kahlil Gibran

In order to make the sale, the next thing you need to do is to build rapport. I cannot stress that enough. Rapport is so important. And remember, you want to have a spark of that passion—that you care about your customer as well as your product.

Rapport starts at the door if you're working retail. It starts with the way you say, "Hello," on the phone. Remember Renée Zellwegger's character in the film *Jerry Maguire?* "You had me at hello."

Once you build the rapport, you have that connection with your customer. And once you have it, you're on your way. You're on the right path. It's awesome! Things are just going to happen.

If you lose the rapport, you lose the connection; and it's not going to happen. So you always have to remember to stay positive and connected to your customer.

Staying positive and upbeat is the key. If you walk onto the salesroom floor and greet somebody like, "What's up?" it's not going to happen. You have to stay upbeat and positive. It has to be, "Hi there! How's your day going?"

Let's think back to when someone was trying to sell *you* something. Would you rather buy from a positive salesperson or a negative one? Of course you would want to buy something from a positive salesperson. You now believe in the product. You're passionate about it because the salesperson truly believes in the product.

Why stay positive? It's much better than being negative! You see where I'm going? Let's start with "Hello." Do you realize the way you start with hello can either make or break a sale? It's really amazing.

So let's practice. Put down the book and practice in your mirror: Hello. Hellooooo. Heh-llo.

If you say it too flippantly, they'll look at you like, "Are you out of your gourd?!" If you do it authentically, they'll be happy to talk to you.

Yes, the way you say hello—actually the way you approach somebody—either on the phone or when they walk in the door determines whether or not you're going to make the sale. You must realize that. Maintaining a positive attitude can make any sale happen! So when you say hello to somebody on the phone, you're going to be as upbeat as you possibly can—again, without going into overdrive. You're passionate, not silly.

Another purpose of this book—along with making you successful—is to keep you upbeat. You must be passionate, so you have to be energized. I want to make you realize that we sometimes get complacent. We assume that person isn't going to buy or we're not going to sell to that person. Remember, you cannot ever make that assumption again.

We can never assume that we're not going to get the sale, no matter what it is. We need to always have that passion and positivity at every single sales opportunity. It's a passion to provide what the customer needs, as well as a passion to make that connection. You never know if they're going to love you so much that they refer you to their friends or family. See chapter 14 on closing the sale and referrals.

Developing rapport is so crucial to sales. If you like me, you're going to continue reading this book. If you like me, you're going to buy something from me. That's what I mean by staying true to yourself because people can see through you.

And what I mean by developing rapport is, again, in the way you say, "Hello." The way you say, "Hi." The way you talk. If you're in a retail setting, that's when the smile on your face comes into play—immediately.

You don't want them to catch you thinking. You should have a smile on your face before they even catch your eye. You don't want their first impression of you to be a scowl, so be happy that you're their opportunity to match them with the right product.

Even if you just lost a customer, do you want the next one seeing you in your mini pity-party? It just means that it wasn't the right fit, so keep on smiling.

You've got to smile automatically, even when you're answering the phone. Why? They can tell you appreciate their call. They literally can hear the smile and the passion in your voice. It really sets the tone for a successful phone sale. Read on for more information about phone sales.

Let's take another look in the mirror and practice your smile. Now frown. Look in the mirror and smile again. You tell me, what do you like better? It doesn't matter what you feel like.

Nobody cares about the day you had—about the night you had before. Nobody cares how many sales you've made in the past or even today—how many sales you don't make. They certainly don't want to be known as a number in your quota!

What they care about is that you honestly and sincerely appreciate them because they may buy something from you. You're passionate about providing true service, so smile! Remember it's all about the customer's needs!

Everyone is looking out for themselves, and you have to be able to read a customer's wants, needs, everything about them. You have to sell them the value of the product. Remember, it's really all about them. It's all about the customer's needs.

It's as simple as that joke about meeting Mr./Ms. Right. Some say, "It's Mr. Right-Now." You are only invested in the customer that you have right in front of you at any given moment. Don't spend a single thought on anyone but them, and you'll make more sales!

As you read through this book, I'll be giving you a wealth of hints and tips in your sales process, like knowing your product and inventory, in order to gain your customer's trust. You're helping them find a product that fits their needs. It's all a win-win situation, but you have to follow the steps in order. So having established the rapport, we go on to making a solid connection with your customer.

Chapter 6: Connection

*Spread love everywhere you go. Let
no one ever come to you without
leaving happier.—Mother Teresa*

*At times our own light goes out and is
rekindled by a spark from another
person. Each of us has cause to think
with deep gratitude of those who
have lighted the flame within us.
—Albert Schweitzer*

*Make new friends,
but keep the old.
One is silver,
the other is gold.
—Girl Scouts*

One thing that's really important for you to be successful is the word "connection". If you don't have a connection with your customer, they really won't have trust in you. Forming a connection actually begins with the nonverbal signals, like smiling.

I really can't stress enough how important it is to smile at people; otherwise, they make all these predeterminations of what you're thinking. A simple smile will erase any preconceived feelings that they have about you. A smile means warmth and acceptance and so many things. Just sit back for a minute, smile, and see how much better you feel.

Sometimes we have to practice the simple act of smiling. I know I said it once before, to practice smiling into a mirror, but it's a useful tool. So pull out a mirror or compact out of your purse or briefcase, right now. And smile. And then frown. And smile. And then frown. Do you like yourself better when you smile? Of course you do! No matter how you're feeling, you need to keep that smile!

That's how your customers see you with a smile. Get it? It's their first impression of you. They're not going to buy from you if you greet them with a frown. Would you buy from a salesperson with a frown? We often forget about the smile when we go into stores.

Think about it. When you go into stores to buy something for yourself, you're looking for that smile. You're looking for that greeting. *"Hi!"* Can you tell that I'm smiling? *Always!* When I greet a customer, I'm always smiling, no matter how busy I am. Even if I'm on the phone and I'm busy with another customer, they can still hear the smile in my voice.

The ultimate goal when we greet a customer is for them to leave our store—or wherever you may be selling—with a bag, a signed invoice, or something tangible. And we forget that, because we let the outside—or whatever—come in to affect our attitude. It's mind boggling.

Waking up on the wrong side of the bed can determine your day. Don't let that happen! Please don't let that happen! At the end of the day—when you make a sale, the feeling is awesome. I love it. So smile!

Let's get back to the connection and starting off with a smile. You really want to connect with your customer so they can trust you. There are so many ways to connect; for example, making sure to do your homework on your customer. We'll cover listening skills later in your steps, but what I'm talking about is that you need to start from the top in determining what they need. Take mental notes on everything they provide—and this will keep your connection flowing.

The key part of that connection is listening to their needs, no matter what you're selling. Your customer needs to see the value before they are able to make a buying decision. If they feel they are being talked in to buying something, they will probably return it or spread the word to never come back. You don't want that to happen, do you?

Selling is really a huge puzzle, and how you connect the pieces determines whether you'll make the sale or not. For example, if you skip part of the selling process, you probably won't be too successful in closing the sale. That's why it's so important to make the right connection at the beginning, and it starts with a smile.

There are so many ways to connect after the smile. Some people say greet with a handshake. Some people don't like a handshake. No matter what, after you say hello people will start sensing if you are genuine or not. Isn't that amazing? Always remember that first smile can set the tone of how the sale will ultimately go.

Deborah says that even people going on auditions are now being told not to go up to shake hands, unless the casting director is offering their hand. They may be seeing a hundred or more people in a day, though, so use your common sense.

And always be true to yourself about that because handshakes can come across as fake. You don't want that to happen as you really want to make sure that you connect with people in the most positive way.

People can be turned off instantly by the wrong connection, and it's hard to reconnect. Think about the last time that you were trying to buy something and you didn't have a connection with that salesperson. You may have left the product there. Or you may have bought the item. It probably wasn't a pleasant buying experience because of the lack of connection that you felt.

I just want to make sure that you really understand how important that it is to connect. There are so many more pieces to the puzzle of successfully, honestly, and trustfully making the sale.

You want returns of happy former customers and referrals because you connected well. You really want the people leaving your retail establishment knowing that their needs were met.

Customers like a professional, passionate salesperson. The customer should feel like you took care of them. The ideal goal is to feel like when they met you, they were meeting a new, genuine friend.

Chapter 7: Greeting

How glorious a greeting the sun gives
the mountains!—John Muir

There is no friend like an old friend
who has shared our morning days, no
greeting like his welcome, no homage
like his praise.—Oliver Wendell Holmes, Jr.

Don't tell your friends about your
indigestion. How are you is a greeting,
not a question.—Arthur Guiterman

I want to explain the greeting. Basically when you greet somebody, you have to stay as positive as possible. You probably know much of what I'm going to talk about, but I want to reinforce it as a tool.

The most important part of the greeting in any kind of sales (retail, outside, and even inside sales, done over the phone) is the smile. On the phone it will boost your vocal quality to sound more cheerful. In many inside sales and customer service representatives' desks, you will find small mirrors on cubicle walls to remind the rep to smile.

You have to smile. Smiling is so important for gaining a customer's trust and rapport. And your smile really does come across, over the phone, in your voice. A customer really can tell when you're smiling.

I know you already practiced, but too often we forget to keep that smile going. I'm not saying keep a fixed smile on your face. Just stay upbeat and positive even when the sale may not be going well.

Building rapport is so important—connecting to that person—and it all starts with the smile. Trust me on this. I've done many seminars where I will actually stop, and if there are *five* or five *hundred* people, I will not go on until everyone in the audience smiles. That's how important it is to smile.

Please take this part of the greeting, the connection, and building rapport seriously. A simple smile will get you in the door. It will get your customer to buy from you if they're walking into a retail store. I cannot stress the importance of a simple smile. It makes the customer feel welcome.

This is why we have sales associates in clothing stores, meandering through the racks—greeting the customer saying, "Hello! Let me know if I can help you find anything." A customer likes to have the salesperson acknowledging their presence. The customer shouldn't have to seek you out if you're not with another customer. And even if you are, you'll say, "Thank you for coming in. I'll be right with you!"

And then the salesperson should always stay at the ready, looking for the buyer's signal to try something on for size.

Back to the greeting, when you smile you feel better about yourself. It releases the tension. Prior to even walking into the store for the day, you should drop your shoulders, take a deep breath, smile, and then walk in the door.

What people care about is their needs, not necessarily what you are selling. They may be walking into your store or calling you on the phone, not really knowing exactly what they want. It all starts with the greeting. I hope you're smiling now!

I can't say it enough: If you are passionate about your job and your product, then you are more likely to sell it than the next person. And you may not believe this, but a smile signifies passion. A frown or a straight face doesn't. If you are passionate about your product, you will sell it with a smile.

You're going to see that the entire selling process ties in together. For those who think they can skip a step, they are sadly mistaken if they think shortcuts will get them there. You're not going to walk up to a customer and say, "What are you buying?" You're going to say, "Hello." You're not going to walk up to a customer without smiling, because smiling sets the tone for the sale.

I saw a commercial on TV and it said, "The average person smiles more than five times a day!" If you're an above average salesperson, this should be natural.

So once you've established that you're in a good mood, you're motivated and you want to make the sale, you have to establish your greeting. Once again, the first thing you do is to what? Smile! Any book or video you've seen about the rapport and greeting, it's all about the smile.

And if you think it seems weird to practice your smile, it really isn't. Why do you think there are a lot of salespeople that don't make the sales? It's because they don't smile or their smile is not genuine. It needs to be authentic because you're happy to help your customer. Be real and absolutely genuine.

Another thing that Deborah shared with me is that smiling is not always a natural thing, especially when your brain is churning. She said that in musical theatre directors constantly have to remind the actors, dancers and singers to smile in rehearsals, as they're just so busy thinking.

The performers are so busy working on all the dance steps and songs that they forget that they're supposed to exude happiness. So just throw off the worries and other nagging thoughts, and just remember to connect genuinely with your customer. We may also be thinking of making our sales goals, so we always have to be cognizant of smiling.

Just think about it. The most important people smile. Look at the president of the United States—especially on the campaign trail and with foreign dignitaries. The president smiles, unless it's a serious issue. It's important to establish that tone right off the bat. I cannot stress that enough.

When you greet your customer, you smile and say, "Hi! How are you?" We may be all caught up in the next step, and we're over-thinking. But it's the simplest thing. Always remember to smile when you say hello.

Chapter 8: Listening

Pretend that every single person you
meet has a sign around his or her
neck that says, "Make me feel
important."—Mary Kay Ash

We have two ears and one mouth so
that we can listen twice as much as
we speak. –Epictetus

Character is much easier kept than
recovered.—Thomas Paine

A very important part of the sales process is often forgotten, and that is actively listening—not just hearing them speak, but actively listening—to your customer. Listening is an art, and it's about receiving and interpreting versus just receiving.

Most salespeople like to hear themselves talk, so they often forget to listen. If you listen to your customer, they will literally tell you everything you need to know about them. But often, salespeople are so quick to interrupt.

Hopefully this isn't you! You may think you know it all. You may think you have the sale. You may think you know what they're going to say and can actually kill the sale before you even start. If you're really listening, you can also pick up on smaller cues toward what the customer needs, as well as what they want.

It's amazing. If you're not making the sales, I challenge you to think back to scenarios or stories that you have that worked in the past. The bottom line is that you most likely talk too much.

And if you stop yourself and really truly listen, the customer will tell you exactly what they need. There are so many stories I can share with you, just on the topic of listening.

Keep in mind, you must not answer the question you ask them. Let the customer answer the question. I have to repeat it— please, don't answer the question you ask them! That drives me crazy! If you already think you know the answer, why ask it? Be patient!

One very memorable time I was doing a jewelry sales seminar, and the owner decided to attend. I didn't want to put him on the spot, but he actually put himself on the spot! This particular session was during a listening skills seminar. And what you had to do in the seminar was learn how to listen.

As funny as it sounds, they all realized something huge at the end of the seminar—they were not really listening to the customer. They learned a lot and admitted that it was a fact that they really just needed to hear themselves talk. If there was no conversation at all, they would talk about something not even pertinent to the business. A little small talk is okay to connect to your customer, but not at the expense of forgetting to listen to their buying signals. You'll see more about this in the communication chapter.

I asked my students, "How often do you ask a question, without really listening to the answer, and five minutes later you ask the same question?" That's a total turnoff to a customer because as simple as it may sound, they can tell that you're not really listening.

Remember me saying something about an automatic disconnect maneuver? That's a definite disconnect! And the whole point of the process in this lesson was for a salesperson to listen to their customer's needs.

So we were doing some role playing. I was playing the customer's role while the owner played the salesperson's role. He greeted me, and it was fine. He proceeded to ask me what my needs were. I said, "Well, it was my anniversary. I'm a couple days late, and I need to get a gift."

He showed me a few things, and I said, "This is nice. That's nice," looking at the jewelry. Within five minutes of the exercise of the selling process, the owner asked the question again, "So what brings you in the store today?" I stopped, and I looked at him and had to ask, "You are kidding, right?" He said, "No. What brings you in the store today?"

I said, "You asked me that question five minutes ago. I told you it was my anniversary and..." He said, "Oh, right!"

Well in front of everyone, he forgot. And this was a role-playing exercise I was doing in front of his staff. He chose to be a volunteer. So if the owner isn't listening, is he really sure he wants to be in sales? As a recap, please remember that listening is an extremely important part of the sale.

One thing that will help you to stay on track with the reason the customer would be in the store is to ask them for more details about the event they're buying the item for. If it's their anniversary and you're selling jewelry, ask them how long they've been married. This helps not only in engaging and maintaining your connection, but with the qualifying questions, in getting something more special if it's a big anniversary.

Again, this helps you to listen better and have a more meaningful conversation with your customer. You may even remember the next time they come in, so you can ask, "So how did your husband enjoy his anniversary gift?" That scores even more bonus points for you in your customers' eyes!

The bottom line is that if you're asking qualifying questions—which is coming up later in the book—without listening, it's going to be a very slow day in your sales. It can make or break a deal and save a lot of frustration if you'll just listen to your customer.

And as always, if you listen thoroughly, and play the steps right, it may mean referrals later. Read on.

Chapter 9: Communication/How Conversations Increase Sales

Don't mumble your life away.
—Ethan Lipton

If you're arguing with a fool, make
sure he isn't doing the same thing.
—Unknown

Think about it. It's not selling. It's communicating!

You want to *change the behavior* in your objecting customers! You want them to *buy*, and your quickest route to that goal is to communicate with the customer. Just talking to them will open the doors of objection! That's as simple as I can make it for you!

Just try it! If you don't, you'll never know how easily it works. Sales is all about communication with your customer. Communication is synonymous with the word "selling." It's the way you communicate.

We will cover objections later, but the point is that communicating can help in all of the steps. Communication is the biggest key to all successful sales. I can't stress enough how important it is to communicate well on any level, both personal and professional. I can see you sitting there, reading and rolling your eyes at this point, in agreement that it makes complete sense.

Why is it so hard for some people to communicate? Why is it so hard to ask questions? Why is it so hard to verbalize your feelings? Why is it so hard to ask your customer to let you know what they're thinking in order for you to help them to be more content by selling them the right item? Why is it so hard to ask for the sale?

So many people I've trained have said, "It's so hard for me to ask somebody for the sale." I just don't understand that. Communication is key to everyone's success. Once there is a communication breakdown, the sales process stops flat. You can't skip any of the steps in the selling process. Communication is key to making you successful in doing all of the steps.

For example, if you can't communicate a greeting, then you're not going to make a sale. If you can't ask the customer questions, how can you qualify them for what they need? If you don't find out what the objections are, you won't make a sale. As you're reading this you need to understand—this is not just a suggestion—this is what you need to do!

If you have terrible communication skills, you need to rectify that. The way that you fix this issue is to practice. You practice on your boss, your family, your friends and your customers. People are just afraid to communicate. They don't want to be rebuffed or seem silly in asking a question. I just don't get it! You need to get over it and just ask them a simple question!

There are so many reasons and excuses—which I'll go into later in chapter 15—that people give me in the seminars. They are afraid to communicate. They don't want to sound stupid. They don't want to ask questions. They're afraid that if they didn't listen to something that a customer already said, they'll repeat a question and upset the customer.

It all ties into staying true to yourself, acting like yourself. In reality, you would normally just say "What?" or you might say "Can you repeat that?" So why can't you ask that of a customer? Again, if you're really listening you won't have to ask them to repeat something that you should have heard. Still, if you didn't catch it—don't lose the sale by being afraid to simply ask again.

This is unlike my role-playing store owner, who simply forgot because he wasn't listening. He embarrassed himself, but if you simply didn't hear it, there's no harm, no foul in asking, "I'm sorry, but could you tell me again?" This may be a good lesson to improve your listening skills.

Another more powerful way of thinking about this is that you're just affirming what the customer said. Instead of being a timid salesperson asking them to repeat themselves, you're just rephrasing what the customer said. This shows the customer that you're listening.

Having confidence in yourself will help you achieve the ability to ask questions. It all boils down to being able to ask the customer to repeat him or herself, as you're just affirming what they said.

I understand when you're in inside sales you can't see the body language. But you can definitely hear the body language. You can hear it in the tone of their voice over the phone. You can tell if they're interested or not, and it's all in your approach to keep their interest.

Again, communication is very important. It's both a skill and an art, and again, it's all in the approach of communicating.

So don't be afraid. If I was afraid, I wouldn't be a successful salesperson. If I was afraid, I wouldn't be writing this book.

As a sales trainer, I am not afraid to ask a customer what they're thinking. I'm not afraid to ask a customer to buy something. I'm not afraid to ask a customer anything that pertains to the product they want to buy or to the sale.

I know if I don't do everything possible to make the sale, someone else is going to sell it to them and I'll lose the commission. So I know I can simply ask the customer, "What are you thinking about? What do you really want? What are you looking for?"

This has nothing to do with confidence or insecurity but with the ability to be an effective communicator. I want you to really sit back and think about your communication comfort level.

You need to determine whether or not you are an effective communicator. If you know you are, you can go on to the next section; but if not, you need to work on this skill. You need to learn how to communicate. And again, the way that you learn to communicate better is through practice.

Deborah told me that this really helps actors to critique themselves in performance, and that is very similar to what we do as salespeople. We want to come across naturally and effectively. You can also role-play at home with this.

If you are with a person and their body language is showing that they're mad or sad, you know you don't have to ask, "What are you thinking?" You can ask, "Are you having a good day? Is everything alright? I hope you're not angry."

The customer may unload on you, and they may be honest. They'll tell you everything if you ask it right. And getting them off of their edgy mood onto one where they feel that they have found a sounding board puts them in a headspace much better to make a choice in buying from you. Now they know you just want the best for them because they can relate to you.

If you're being real and identifying or empathizing with them, they'll feel it if you approach it the right way. Sometimes they bring in with them anger or some other baggage that they already had—it may have been from the salesperson that angered them at another store. You may get the customer with the chip on their shoulder.

You never know if you're going to end up having a Kleenex moment like the commercials. Okay, so your customers most likely aren't actors. But if you communicate with them and show that you can relate to them, they're going to be in your corner. You don't want to be an actor either, although when you are selling, it's your stage. You need to be real. You want to be yourself with them, and they'll just feel like you understand them.

I know that a lot of what you're reading in this book is repetitious. Unless you see it and read it all the time, you're not going to get the point. We often skip too much and may not retain a lot of what we read. We tend to read the parts we want to read. And a lot of times we just skim and read the parts that seem significant to us.

Every part of this book relates to every step of the sale. Each part of this book will make you a successful salesperson. And you really have to understand that. Once you understand that, then you'll be a successful salesperson as you incorporate these lessons.

So again, you must work on the art of communication. Practice it, over, and over and over again. Practice it, especially with your customers. You can even tell your customer you're working on communicating better. They really appreciate honesty.

Customers want an honest salesperson. They don't want a fake. I can't tell you this enough. You must work on communication. I will be giving you more examples as you read on.

Let's say you're with a customer and they're not talking. They're just not giving you anything. Most of you reading this book have had one of those customers who are just not talking. My best suggestion to you is to find some common ground with your customer. When you do that, they'll really open up. When the customer knows they can relate to you, it's easier to communicate. And that goes both ways.

You can comment on what they're wearing. If they're wearing a shirt with fish, you can ask, "So when was the last time you went fishing? Were they biting? What lures did you use?" If they're wearing a sports team jersey, you say, "Oh wow! You're a Washington Wizards fan? They're having a great season!" Or it might be, "How'd you like the game last night. Boy, I didn't think that player was going to make that shot!"

Find that common ground with your customers, even if they were already talking to you in the first place. It's amazing how you can have someone walk in with a long face and establish some common ground with them. You never know, like I said in the connections chapter, if you're going to meet your new best friend.

Communication is a wonderful tool to establish common ground with customers. Isn't that fantastic?! And nothing shows passion like rooting for the same team. Then you just transfer that passion to the sales process.

I'd like to make sure that you know that understanding your customers is very important. I want to caution you, though. Often when we're listening to our customers or prospects in stating their reason to buy things, we sometimes answer them saying, "I understand." But let me ask you, do you really understand? "Understand" is really not a word you want to use lightly.

Say that somebody is explaining a story that happened to them from their past. And we're doing a good job, not interrupting them. Unless you really have been there with them or lived their experience, how can we really say that we understand? You may say you feel their frustration. You can apologize for their sadness over what happened to them. Saying that you understand may offend some customers, even if that's not your intent.

Let's take as an example when my mom passed away. People would say, "I'm sorry for your loss. I understand." I would look at them and say, "How can you say, 'I understand.' This is my mom. If you had the exact same relationship with your mom and you don't have her anymore, then you could say you understand."

It's very important that you don't go there as it can make some people react in a very defensive manner, and that can shut your sale down very quickly. Again, you can empathize, but some people are very sensitive over this kind of issue.

Here's another thing to make you think. There is actually a fundraiser called "Walk a Mile in Her Shoes" which benefits survivors of domestic violence and rape. Men actually walk a mile in high heels to get an idea of the pain that women experience in their lives. At least it makes them *think*, but they still wouldn't know what child birth or domestic violence is like. Again, you can't really understand something fully if you haven't gone through what your customer has experienced.

So really think about this as you're reading. And the next time that you go out to buy something and the salesperson says, "I understand. I totally understand." Ask them, "Do you really? Have you lived that experience?"

You've got keep in mind, there's so much to being a great salesperson, but we often think ten steps ahead. Are you living in the moment? Are you really living in the moment—on the same step, as the customer?

We really don't listen thoroughly when we're thinking so many steps ahead. If we're not listening to our customer, we're really not selling the value of the product. You could even be selling them the wrong product if you haven't been listening to their answers.

Think about it. Really think about how the process ties together if you follow it correctly. But so often we either speak too quickly, interrupt people when they're talking—or worse, we're not listening. Again, this means we're not selling the value.

And even worse than not listening is when we're answering the question we ask them ourselves. I know I'm repeating it, but that drives me crazy! Sales people are so darned impatient sometimes. Your customer needs time to think of an answer. Do not, I repeat, do not rush them. You'll gain their respect if you let them answer your questions on their own.

I don't want to be a downer here, but do you fit this picture? If you do, you really need to think about it and think about ways of changing and how to follow the process so you can be better at your job.

Keep the communication going, and keep it positive!

Chapter 10: Qualifying

If you're going to help a man, you
want to know something about him,
don't you?— Joseph, character from
It's a Wonderful Life

Do what you can to do what you
ought, and leave hoping and fearing
alone.—Thomas Henry Huxley

Quailify *verb,* -fied, -fy·ing. **1.** to provide with proper or necessary skills, knowledge, credentials, etc.; make competent: *to qualify oneself for a job.* **2.** to modify or limit in some way; make less strong or positive: *to qualify an endorsement.*

Qualifying is part of the sale process, asking questions to determine what your customer's buying power is and what they both want and need. It is finding out what product you can successfully match them up with. You could also think of it as giving the customer info so they're fully informed about your product.

If you don't know your product well, it may cost you the sale. Keep in mind that customers do their homework too. They are very savvy these days when it comes to checking out things they want to buy. When they enter your store they are looking for great customer service and value. Then the cost shouldn't matter. If you qualify their needs, they will see the value and buy it!

Objections aren't necessarily a bad thing. When somebody objects to something, they're still interested. It just narrows them into the right product for their buying power and especially their needs. You are helping them to find the right fit.

The art of qualifying a customer is determining what questions to ask them. The most important part of qualifying is listening to your customer, as we covered so thoroughly in chapter 8. We all know that we're guilty of not listening as intently as we should. Listening is such an important part of the sale. Can I say it enough? You've got to listen to your customer to get the qualifying clues. And remember what I said about talking less and more listening?

You can't be doing all the talking, all the time: 1. The customer gets bored. 2. They think you're not interested in them or their needs. So you have to take a balanced approach. Again, as I said before in chapter 8, make sure to really listen to their questions and their answers so that you can quickly qualify them, pointing them in the right direction in the sale process.

You have to sell yourself, sell your product, and do your homework, too. There are so many aspects to qualifying, and you have to be good at it to be successful. After you initially greet your customer—depending on what the situation is—if it's a retail customer coming into your store, you need to know what questions to ask.

You also need to know your inventory, the location of the inventory and where to take the customer in your store. Phone orders are only a bit easier. You still have to have all that knowledge, but you're not seeing the customer face-to-face or having to walk them to the product. If you have that down— knowing your inventory and various products lines that will fit their needs—you gain the trust of the customer.

Trust from your customer is a very important part of a sale. Along with confidence on your part, trust is a key element to making a sale. And if you've correctly qualified them for the right product, they are much more likely to return to you or your store or give you referrals.

You really need to prepare yourself, whether it's retail or wholesale, even when you go knocking on doors. You need to know ahead of time what questions to ask. People are pretty savvy these days. They can easily go on the internet and do their own research. Most times, I have to say, they've done their homework before their appointment with you. So you'd better do your homework before you see them.

 One of Deborah's friends actually works on knowing more than the salesperson when she's going to buy cars and other big purchases. So knowing your product is very important these days. She actually looks at what service may cost in the long run and how the part prices compare to other cars. That way, she feels she's fully informed in her choice.

It's also a confidence booster for you to know way ahead of time about your product—even new releases coming soon. Let's say, for example, you're selling jewelry. You need to know the stones, and you need to know the birthstones of the month.

No matter what you're selling, customers like confident, knowledgeable salespeople. Remember, most of all, customers really like it when you're genuine versus fake or putting on a show. They really can tell these days! So be real.

I can remember twenty-five years ago when you could easily bluff or muscle your way through for a quick sale without really knowing the product. But these days, customers really know their stuff.

When it comes to qualifying a customer, it does help to be on the ball. It really makes you more credible and successful. We haven't even touched on the idea of closing a sale, but your qualifying questions are so important to know ahead of time. You're much more likely to sell your product when you know it inside and out.

This really ties into listening to your customer because identifying your customer's needs is such an important aspect of the sale. There are so many salespeople who forget. I'm going to repeat it–to drive the point home–they forget to listen to the customer. That's unbelievable and unacceptable when it comes to sales and qualifying customers!

When you have to ask a question, how embarrassing is it when the customer says, "I just told you the answer to that"? Remember my role-playing store owner in chapter 8? There goes your credibility—down ten notches in my eyes.

You should ask if you really didn't hear it the first time, but you *really* have to be *prepared to listen*. Make a mental list of your customer's answers. The more you pay attention, the more info you have for your list.

It all ties into making the sale and really doesn't matter what you're selling. Listening while qualifying makes the sale a much more pleasant experience—for both you and your customer. And you're so much more likely to sell your product.

They'll remember you and come back for repeat business—and they'll even refer you to friends and/or family—if you genuinely show your customers that you care about them.

Chapter 11: Buying Signals

Here's your sign.—Bill Engvall

Sometimes we search for signs, and they're already in front of us. You don't even have to ask for them. It's literally like there is a truck full of different signs falling out in front of us. We're still looking for them, asking for them, all the while driving around the obvious signs.

It's like the cliché, "You wouldn't see the sign unless you were hit with it upside the head." It's that way with customers, too. Bottom line: Start listening to your customer—they are giving you all the signs you need.

Once you master buying signals, it's fairly easy going. A lot of salespeople don't realize how important buying signals are. See figure 1 for a list.

Buying Signals:

Verbal

- Asking about the product
- How much is it?
- What credit cards do you take?
- Do you offer financing?
- Inquiring more information about the company
- Asking if there is a contract

Non Verbal

- Smile
- Nodding
- Pen in hand
- Reaching for their wallet
- Change in their voice
- Change in posture

Figure 1

They really don't think about it or put it together early enough in the sales process. I'm not sure why, but I think it's really important because it's part of listening and observing body language in your customer. Listening is key to being a successful salesperson. How can you determine what they want if you're not really listening to their signals?

Buying signals really start when someone opens the door and they want to buy something from your store. I know you're thinking, the steps all seem to overlap each other in what you need to do and all that you need to look for. Again—I can't stress it enough—don't skip any of it or you'll miss the important signals coming out of the process. So watch for the signals they give out upon coming into your store.

And watch for the signals when they answer the phone, "Hello." Amazing isn't it? We don't even think about it. I've taught so many people to listen and watch out for buying signals, and they didn't initially even realize what a buying signal was. It's so easy. When someone asks about something, it's a buying signal.

If you really sit back and think about it, you can target the buying signals and use them later in the sales process. It's like a behavioral-science experiment for you because you can see how easy it really is!

You are more apt to make a sale when listening for their signals. So, for example, if someone stops in your television store and they ask, "Where are your Toshiba televisions?" What would you be thinking? Well, what I would be thinking is "This person wants to buy a Toshiba."

But I've had so many people in class say, "Well what I would be thinking is, 'They just want to look at a Toshiba.'" My answer to them is always, "How can you think that when you are a salesperson? You are there to sell your product." So let's go back.

A customer walks in and they ask, "Where are the Toshibas?" You immediately say, "Right over here. Please follow me." If you hesitate, trying to remember where your product is and do not know your inventory, you're less apt to make the sale. Knowing the location of all of your inventory shows credibility.

Credibility is so important. Remember the store owner's faux pas in our role playing when he forgot why I was in there? His credibility as a salesperson was diminished in my eyes because he forgot my signal.

Most salespeople never really realize how important buying signals are to the sales process. They don't even know what buying signals are, yet it's a good listening and observational technique to learn from. Observe as you say hello to a customer. Even the way they say hello to you is a buying signal.

If they're standoffish, they might be saying, "I'm just looking." They're still there, so you might as well sell something to them! Just keep reading the signals. If they're looking at TVs, they're most likely going to be buying one soon, and shouldn't it be from you? So just keep listening and observing them as they browse.

If you can really understand a buying signal, then it will make your job a lot easier to close a sale. Salespeople take buying signals for granted. A buying signal is so important and easy to attain. If you really think about it, all customers, no matter what you're selling, give off buying signals.

You might think of your customers like bats. They navigate off of echolocation. They just send off this signal, naturally, to be able to fly and find their food. Customers are the same with their buying signals. If you watch for these signs, you'll be able to read them and steer them toward the right product.

Even an objection is a buying signal. If somebody doesn't want to buy something, but they're not leaving or hanging up on the phone, they're giving you a signal that you should analyze. Maybe it's just hesitation in making their choice. They could very well be analyzing products, while you analyze them!

If someone truly doesn't want to buy something, they'll walk out or they'll hang up the phone. So a buying signal really starts out from "Hello."

Again, just like the girl in *Jerry Maguire*, "You had me at hello." Sometimes it just works, but you always have to follow the buying signals to determine what the customer really wants.

So do you have what it takes? Do you understand what buying signals are? You can learn from each kind of the examples in the list so that you may also know how to counter objections, with a sincere nod to the customer to tell them you understand what they are saying.

It's really important to know that an objection doesn't necessarily mean "No". It may just mean that you have to narrow them down to the right product that fits their needs—budget and otherwise. You can still counter their objection to point them in the right direction, or they need a minute to figure out how they will pay for the item.

Many times it's not you if they're not buying. The timing may not be right. It's beyond your control. You don't want to seem desperate because you want them coming back when they are ready.

Don't be desperate as that will turn a customer off immediately. And just be yourself. Just be you—a passionate, helpful, caring salesperson, and hopefully you'll sell them what they were looking for when they are ready to buy.

Go ahead! Give them your card and tell them to ask for you by name, knowing you are hoping to fit them with the perfect match.

Chapter 12: Objections

The greater the tension, the greater is the potential. Great energy springs from a correspondingly great tension of opposites. —Carl Jung

I was taught that the way of progress is neither swift nor easy. —Marie Curie

Being defeated is often a temporary condition. Giving up is what makes it permanent. — Marilyn vos Savant

Most sales writers label this next part of the sales process as "overcoming objections." I don't particularly agree with this way of thinking. Everyone realizes that objections have to be overcome, but an objection isn't necessarily a bad thing. It can be as simple as a signal that it's not the right product. They haven't been sold the value yet.

Please keep in mind, when a customer is objecting to something and they're still there, they really are interested. They are simply giving you signals that they're not settled on the right product quite yet. Obviously, they haven't left. They really just want more information or help in figuring out how they can buy the product.

So to say "to overcome an objection" is only partly accurate. It's actually their way of qualifying us, to see if they are getting the right product for the right price.

An objection is just an objection. Note that I didn't call it rejection. You need to learn how to deal with an objection such as those on figure 2—knowing how to correctly answer their questions. Hopefully you can flush out objections by finding out what their needs are, what is truly important to them.

It could be as simple as reading your customer's body language. Are they fidgeting? There are so many studies out there on body language. If they put their hands in their pockets, it means one thing; if they fold their arms, it means another.

Let's not get so technical. You should be able to understand people's objections by reading your customer's actions and reactions. You should be able to read their

Buying Signals Showing Objection:

Verbal

- I am just shopping right now.
- I'm not buying right now.
- I'm just looking.
- Thanks, but no thanks.
- Do you have something a little more economical?
- This doesn't fit in my budget.
- I'm not "in the market" right now, but just researching.

Body Language

- Avoiding eye contact
- Handling multiple items and putting them back
- Pulling away

Figure 2

body language as if it's plainly printed on their forehead. Wouldn't that be a funny sight to see?

All over the country, in so many different seminars and class settings, salespeople are telling me that they really are afraid of the objections and asking the customer why they're not buying. It's just mind boggling to me that some salespeople will not ask that question and learn from these objections. You can try the counters to them in figure 3.

> **How to Find and Deal with (Counter) the Objection:**
>
> **Verbal**
>
> - Why are you hesitating?
> - Do you see the value in the product or service? A few minutes ago you did. What changed?
> - Is it truly the price?
> - What questions were not answered?
> - I apologize if I didn't give you all the information.
> - Let's start over. I want you to see the value.
> - You walked into my store for a reason.
> - Please tell me why you're not buying, so I understand.
>
> **Figure 3**

Why is it so difficult to ask the customer, "Why are you not buying?" It's so easy to ask that. Just practice saying it right now.

Put the book down for a moment and ask aloud, into the mirror, any phrase to counter or overcome the customer's objections. You can choose from a myriad of phrases in figure 3.

Or if you're afraid to ask these questions so directly, try saying, "A penny for your thoughts. I know this sounds silly, but can you tell me what you're thinking? What's stopping you from buying this product?" When you get personal, just being yourself, the customer can relate to you. They will feel free to share why they have an objection, and you will be able to counter with your passion about the product.

You are now a passionate salesperson. Remember this book was written to encourage you. You love your product so your enthusiasm may be enough to overcome objections.

Set the book down again and repeat after me (into the mirror): I am a salesperson! I am confident! From this moment forward—if you haven't been doing it—act like a confident salesperson, and you will be one!

Why?! Why is it so difficult to ask somebody why they're not buying something? Now if you're in a retail operation, somebody can turn right around and walk out the door. If you've got an appointment, somebody can always ask for a different salesperson or they can leave.

Whatever the situation, it doesn't matter. An objection is an objection. It means that somebody is stalling in making a decision. It is up to you to start them up again—fix the hesitation and make the sale.

I've had people in classes and seminars who say, "There's no way I could do that!" or "Oh, my goodness. I couldn't do that! I'd be prying."

I just don't understand it so my response is always, "Okay. They're in your store to buy something. You're there to sell it to them, so how is that prying? So maybe you need some practice." You know, it's okay to need some practice. Practice on your customers!

People say to me, "I can't sell. I don't like rejection." Everyone deals with rejection. It's how you deal with rejection that makes you a better salesperson. It's that simple. Stop making the selling process so difficult. It's really so simple. Again, it's not selling, it's really communicating.

It's not going to break you to ask someone the small questions, or even the big ones, of why they're not buying. The possibility of losing a couple of sales—feeling awkward while learning how to ask the questions—will only be an investment in your newfound chutzpah (audacity)!

Deborah shared with me that in directing new actors, you have to stretch them past their comfort zone. She says some get there more quickly than others. I just need you to stretch into the comfort zone and confidence of asking the questions about the customer's objections.

Now I'm going to break form here and give you a quote that really fits here:

> You have to leave the city of your
> comfort and go into the wilderness of
> your intuition.—Alan Alda

You have to ask the questions, and yes, it may not feel comfortable for you, but you just have to do it. I just don't understand people who say they can't ask the customer for the sale. If you can't ask for the sale, you may want to rethink if sales is the right job for you.

Salespeople are often filled with excuses. "Well, I called them twelve times. I can't call them the thirteenth time." My answer is always, "Well, that other person that called them the thirteenth time got the sale." It's all in the approach—and reaching them when they're at the tipping point of being ready. People know when you're fake. They want to buy from someone they can believe in and trust. And they're going to buy from somebody, so it might as well be from you instead of the next salesperson!

I wanted to share another story about my son, in his outside sales job. He had an appointment with a customer, and she didn't want to hear anything about promotions. They'd had some small talk, and then it got to the specifics of the sale. When he got to that part in the sale, he mentioned promotions.

She said "I hate promotions." She didn't want to hear it, and the main reason was that promotions end and the price of the product goes up. So my son quickly changed tactics and asked if she was happy with her current provider. She said she wasn't happy. That was obvious because she was open to meeting with my son.

He said that it was a good thirty minutes of objections. And my son finally said to her, "I've worked with you for a while. You like our product, and I'm not going to take 'No' for an answer." She accepted the offer, and he made the sale. It was amazing.

Was it that he wore her down? No. Did he prove the value of the product? Yes. It may have taken a while, but she finally saw that there was no way out but to just take the offer. It just made sense to her at that point, and you can't fight common sense!

It really works when you're not afraid of the customer. And if you have a passion for selling and you love your product, then you'll be able to sell it no matter what.

Don't be afraid of your own shadow! Sometimes we just get in our own way. Knock that shadow away, and just ask the questions that will narrow down your customer's choices and objections to what they really do want to buy. Objections are quite simply their filtration process.

My son said that his customer told him what she liked about him. It was the fact that he was real. He was not on a power trip, and he truly cared about helping her business improve by being more efficient. Here he had twenty or thirty minutes of negative conversation. He turned it into a positive and made the sale.

Now would you rather do that or would you give up? There are so many people who would just give up. You don't have to! He developed a rapport with this person, and he went for it. It was just a fantastic story, and of course I was proud of him.

So keep it in mind. You're obviously not going to make every sale, but if you listen to the customer, you'll have an open door to make the sale. And common sense dictates that asking the questions guarantees you more sales than if you don't ask. So just ask the questions!

Remember when the customer said to my son, "I hate promotions"? That was the end of that. It didn't matter anymore. The "promotion" word was out of the conversation. The point is that you never give up. Just don't give up!

Again, you're not going to make every sale, but don't give up at the first objection signal. You may feel like you're being rejected if they're hesitating, giving objections. But if they haven't left—it shows that they're still interested!

Just don't give up. I won't give up telling you to not give up! They're going to buy it from somebody who doesn't give up, so that somebody should be you.

Chapter 13: Overcoming Objections

Obstacles cannot bend me. Every
obstacle yields to effort.
—Leonardo da Vinci

Determination gives you the resolve
to keep going in spite of the
roadblocks that lay before you.
—Denis Waitley

Most of our obstacles would melt away
if, instead of cowering before them, we
should make up our minds to walk
boldly through them.
—Orison Swett Marden

I know that I said in the previous chapter that I don't particularly agree with it being called "overcoming objections," but as you'll see in some of my favorite quotes here, I think of it as molding and sculpting. You can chisel the objections until the perfect fit—of a customer to a product—just happens. It can still be natural and unforced. Leonardo da Vinci had such a way with words and art. It just fit perfectly.

You're still overcoming the objection by whittling away at their soft spoken façade or chipping away at their stone-walled marbleized blocks. You can think of it now as a new art form.

In my travels all over the country, when we start getting to know each other in the training seminars, people tend to open up more. They begin sharing how they really feel and admitting the things they need to do to improve in their sales process. They usually recognize fairly quickly that the objections are one of those areas they need to strengthen.

You may feel it's a never-ending battle to overcome the objections and close the sale. Please keep in mind, by the time you get to that step, hopefully you have developed a rapport. That makes overcoming objections so much easier. Why do I say that? Merely because your customer has not left the building. That's a great signal in itself.

You may chuckle at this right now, but most people don't think about that fact. This fear comes over them, and they think, "Uh oh! The objections are coming, and I won't know what to say."

Now this goes back to listening. So if you forget to listen to their needs, then obviously you're not going to know how to overcome their objections. You need to remember them and be responsive—as quickly as you can so that they know you were listening. Again, this could help in getting referrals if they know you're on the spot.

So let's really think about it. The customer comes in the door. They're looking for something. You approach them and start the selling process. You greet them. You start asking them questions about what brings them into the store today and what their needs are. Then once you establish their needs and identify the right product and sell the value, you're finally able to ask for the sale.

So you ask for the sale, and they say, "Oh! I have no intentions of buying today." Don't you love that one? Then they add the real kicker, "I'm just looking." You freeze and think,

"What do I say?" There may be a ten, twenty or thirty-second pause. There are so many answers to that question.

Objections are either a question or a statement. If your customer makes a statement, you say nothing. You don't want to talk yourself out of a sale. There's no need to answer when they didn't ask a question.

The best tactic that I've found is to just sit back and say nothing, absolutely nothing, and just watch the customer's expression. See who talks first. If the customer talks first, then you'll probably win the sale because you're letting the customer do most of the talking and you're doing most of the listening.

Now if nobody says anything, it may feel like you're at an impasse. So you can ask, "What are you thinking?" When he or she says, "I have no intentions of buying today," again you can ask, "Well what are you thinking about. Why not?" You can reengage over everything that you talked about prior to getting to this point.

For example, they're shopping for a car. They take it for a test drive. They verbalize that it's everything that they wanted. They're very excited about the car and you feel like this sale is in the bag. So you're already thinking about the contract, and you get to the point, "So do you want to finance this, or pay cash?"

And they say, "Oh. I have no intentions of buying today." So you try that silence thing, and it's not working for you because nobody's talking.

I guarantee that somebody will say something because they're still in your showroom! Hopefully it will be the customer first. They may ask, "Why aren't you saying anything?" Keep in mind, this entire time they haven't left the building. If they didn't like you, if they didn't like what they saw, they would have left the building.

So you have every right to start overcoming objections and ask for the sale. It may take four, five, six or maybe even seven times of overcoming objections and asking for the sale. But if you throw in the towel, someone else is going to get the sale. So go back to reengaging.

"I had no intentions of buying anything today. I am just looking around. I just started my shopping." And you say "Hmmm. Well, what are you thinking because five minutes ago, everything was perfect: The color, the accessories, the price. So I'm not sure I understand. Please explain."

Wow! How powerful can that be? The customer has to justify why they're not buying, don't they? They may be trying to stall and haggle with you, to negotiate, and get a better price. But again, they're still there.

You may get numerous replies. The customer might say, "Well I just don't buy the first place I look. I wasn't expecting to spend this much money." So you might come back with, "Now it's like seven or eight minutes ago that you said you didn't mind the price and you would love to just make a deal." In other words, what are you doing? You're actually repeating everything they said to you. You're reengaging with them.

That's why listening is so key to sales. But as I said before, we tend to think two, four, five, ten steps ahead of ourselves in the selling process. And we're not keyed or homed in to the customer's needs.

If you don't listen, you're not going to make the sale. Now you may get lucky sometimes, and the customer might say, "Oh, I'm tired of looking around. I'm just going to buy it." How often does that really happen?

We love those lay-it-down customers, but if it was that easy, we'd all be millionaires. And what we're not doing is: 1. Listening. 2. Reengaging in the right way when the objections start. Agreed?

So live for the moment. Stay in the moment. Listen to your customer. It's kind of fun. Try it. Stop talking. Start listening. You may really start enjoying the sales process. It's a lot less stressful.

Why is it so hard for some of us to just stop talking and let the customer give us their clues? If you're so busy talking, you'll miss the big signals. Sometimes they're like the big red emergency flares. But if we forget to listen and are just yapping, we'll miss those signal-flares.

They will tune you out if you're not talking about what they want to hear. So don't just keep up the small talk if they're not with you. And that's what we tend to do as salespeople. That's why in every book that you pick up and read, almost all the quotes allude to the fact that you need to start listening and stop talking.

Did you read the quote about doing more listening and less talking? If not, review chapter 8 on listening. Did you "hear" what I said?

It bears repeating: Listen to your customers the first time and they'll give you everything you need to know about overcoming their objections. So listen thoroughly from the time they come in your door. That's key to nearly everything in the process. I wouldn't repeat myself unless it mattered. Got it? Good!

Remember, don't skip the steps in sales process! Build the rapport, stay in the moment—being authentic, listen to the customer, and ask for the sale. Sometimes it seems like it's all fused together, but you absolutely cannot skip anything as you'll forget some of the most important steps.

Objections won't happen quite as much if you really listen more. Your customer will say, "Wow! You really listen to my needs!" How often has a customer ever said that to you? It will be a lot from now on. I guarantee that if you take my advice!

Think about it. You have to basically look at everything surrounding your customer, no matter what they're buying. You have to watch their moves, their body language. And really listen to what they're saying. If you don't have eye contact with your customer, they're probably not even listening to you.

Again there's one more powerful thing that will help you in your selling. Passion. If you're passionate about what you're selling, you will definitely make more sales. I feel very strongly about that. You could say I'm passionate about you being passionate about selling, especially when it comes to selling the value of your product!

You know, next time a telemarketer calls your house, don't hang up on them. Listen to those calls. It's very interesting. You can actually tell if they like their job, if they're smiling while they're talking, if they're sitting up straight.

I'm not saying you have to buy, but you can thank them for calling and tell them that you appreciated them sharing what they wanted to sell, but you may not be interested at this time. You can tell if they're "robots," meaning they're robotic in their delivery. Learn from them. Keep it real! And if they were good, learn from that, too.

It could very well be that someone has retired from the sales floor and is now keeping it real on the phone with inside or outside sales or telemarketing, so you could get someone with great experience. And then *you'll* be the one giving *them* the objections!

Chapter 14: Closing The Sale/Referrals

Carpe diem.—Horace

Be happy, happy, happy,
And seize the day of pleasure.
—Robert Frost from "Carpe Diem"

Strike while the iron is hot.
—English proverb

Closing is my favorite part of the selling process! I can't believe people are afraid to ask for the sale. You're afraid of sounding too pushy? No, no, no! Not at all!

People love to be sold—the moment they see the value. Don't you? It's awesome when you finally see why you need the item and how it's going to benefit you. The greatest feeling is when your customer thanks you for helping them make a decision they couldn't make on their own. So please do not be afraid to ask for the sale. If they see the value, the money doesn't matter.

The more confident you are, the better. You gain that confidence. I have so many people on day one of training telling me they have no confidence. And on the last day of training, they leave saying their biggest takeaway is feeling more confident.

I feel like repeating it one-thousand times over and over again. It's the fun part, it really is. If your customer sees the value, they will find a way to purchase the product or service. Trust me! I have taught many people who say on the first day of class, "I'm not comfortable asking people to buy," and by the end of class they can't remember having said that!

Remember at the top of this book that I said we cannot rest on the laurels of our last sale? We all have to work smarter versus harder. So does the sale end here, as soon as you take their cash or swipe their card? No! It's just a window to your next opportunity! Remember, too, I told you I'm a "Tell-it-like-it-is-window-person"?

Maybe it will be a little while until that customer needs another television, but maybe their neighbor will be visiting and impressed with the purchase their friend has made. What better way to grab a new customer than to send home a happy buyer! They're your mouth-piece!

It's time to strike while your iron is hot! Now is the perfect time to get three business cards out of your pocket and say with a flourish, "Now I know you're going to be happy and hopefully not back too soon, but your friends are going to be impressed with your new acquisition. They just need to come see me, and I'll get them all set up, too!"

Referrals and word of mouth are your best advertising, and it's nearly free! You can always go online and print personalized business cards. So there's no excuse for you not having a business card! That reminds me, as my clients in the workshops come armed to the hilt with excuses.

There's no reason for excuses! A very wise man told me if you don't sell it, someone else will!

Chapter 15: No Excuses

None of us is defined by our circumstances, nor are we defined by how other people perceive us. It is up to each one of us to define ourselves, and that is a life's work. Each of us has the ability to lead a dynamic life by pursuing our unique goals and dreams. There are no limits to what you can do.—Stedman Graham

You are the only problem you will ever have and you are the only solution.
—Raymond Douglas Stanford

Change is inevitable, personal growth is always a personal decision.
—Bob Proctor

Worry is like a rocking chair: it gives you something to do but doesn't get you anywhere.—Harry Leslie Stroupe

It's just amazing. I raised my kids, telling them that they've got to be professional when they're out in the world. They have to be passionate about what they do. They can't be complacent at any time. People notice that.

I know, you're probably reading this and saying, "How come those people who are complacent, or call in sick all the time, or yada yada yada, and still have their jobs?"

Well we can all say that life's not fair sometimes, but that doesn't mean that you have to fall prey to that victim mentality. If you stay true to yourself and work hard every day, it will ultimately pay off. I think most of you who are reading this will agree with me. It will ultimately pay off. And again, that ties back into confidence.

You also can't fall prey to the slacker mentality. You don't want to become one of those people who just doesn't care. You need to be passionate, and you know, sometimes you'll have to apologize to a customer. Sometimes, you made a mistake or the ad's wrong.

You have to swallow your pride and say, "You know, I'm very sorry. I'm sorry that you got the wrong information. I'm sorry there weren't enough TVs in the store for the sale." But too many people make excuses, and I think that I could write a whole book on excuses. Really, where do excuses get you? Nowhere—just like that rocking chair quote.

So just accept it and grow from it all. It's not going to work if you stay passive and mired in excuses. Action is so much better than excuses.

People you work for will tend to remember if you're an excuse-maker or a doer. Seriously. Think about it. It makes sense, right? Think about when your boss came up to you with an issue and you just started spilling over with the excuses. Really? Where did it get you?

It doesn't matter whether you say you're sorry or that it won't happen again or you're sorry for the inconvenience. If you know you're wrong, admit it. The stress is over. You don't have to worry about thinking up silly excuses.

It makes sense, doesn't it? Oh, well. I'm new. We just opened. There weren't enough customers. The weather was bad. Don't you think that your boss, bringing up your low sales, already knows that? They just want to see how you react to their question.

I'd like to encourage you to get busy. Think of what we talked about in chapter 14 and setting start goals. Be proactive. What is your plan to increase sales? What is your game plan? Make it happen! Get into action!

Do. Or do not. There is no try. —Yoda, character from Star Wars

I just had to add that one, as Yoda just made so much sense. And that is that. There is absolutely no room for excuses. Only action. So get out there and passionately be yourself and sell the value of your product to your customer. No questions asked- unless it's you asking your prospect what would get them into the frame of mind to get out their checkbook.

And let me know how that's working for you! It's worked for me!

Chapter 16: Goals/Visionary Thinking

Your time is limited, so don't waste it living someone else's life. Don't be trapped by dogma—which is living with the results of other people's thinking. Don't let the noise of others' opinions drown out your own inner voice. And most important, have the courage to follow your heart and intuition. They somehow already know what you truly want to become. Everything else is secondary.—Steve Jobs

Genius is 1 percent inspiration and 99 percent perspiration.—Thomas Edison

Nothing limits achievement like small thinking; nothing expands possibilities like unleashed imagination.
—William Arthur Ward

You have brains in your head.
You have feet in your shoes.
You can steer yourself in
Any direction you choose.
—Dr. Seuss

I just love how Steve Jobs shared that bit of wisdom with the graduating class of Stanford in 2005. Jobs revolutionized Apple Computer, from a sinking ship to a leader in computing, graphics, entertainment and communications. He was such a visionary leader, changing the way we think. But instead of just thinking of what we already had, he was constantly thinking proactively, about what we needed to make life easier and more fun.

That same vision applied to the goals that he had for Apple. It was sad that he went so early, before imparting even more of his wisdom, but the lesson he leaves is a big one. Set sail, and you can chart your course with your vision.

That's kind of what Dr. Seuss said in not so many words, but he did that with *Green Eggs and Ham*, too. It was one of his best sellers, yet he was challenged to write the book using only fifty words. It would be nice if we'd keep from using too many words with our customers, too. If we could have Dr. Seuss' imagination, we could really be visionary!

I've covered the basics of the selling process, but I really want to talk a little bit about goal setting. You've got to be visionary but start with the small ones. I firmly, passionately believe that mini-goals are more realistic than huge goals. Like they say, you can't eat an elephant all at once. You need to do it in bite-sized chunks.

Quite often, we do our New Year's resolutions, but are they really realistic? Are they going to drop like the dinosaurs did before we can get unstuck in our thinking? Or are you really mired in the old way of doing things? How's that working for you? If it was, would you be reading this book?

Admit it. Really. Those New Year's resolutions only last a month or so. The gym. Dieting. Not stressing. Not sweating the small stuff. I could go on and on, but long-range goals are really not so realistic, especially in sales. I know you've heard this again and again, but it's worth repeating.

I don't have statistics, but I've met a lot of people along the way that have given me this same advice. I want to share that advice with you, to personally set those mini-goals—doable, bite-sized attainable ones.

When you're at work you often get those goals set for you as your "quota." Your boss is more than happy to give you a goal if you don't aspire to come up with something concrete on your own.

That can cause a lot of stress, pain and lack of sleep. So you really want to focus on little goals. And keep working toward them, every day, whether it's selling one more item every day than targeted in your former goal or you're making strides to pass your self-appointed quota!

Let me share a personal story with you. My sister was in a sales slump. She was setting this huge goal for herself and it actually changed her attitude because it wasn't realistic. She wasn't real positive and she wasn't enthusiastic in her inside sales position. It came across in her selling.

She'd dropped in one morning before work. We talked about it and she said, "I'm really getting worried. I'm not making my numbers. I'm not hitting my goals. I don't know what's wrong."

Now my sister is an excellent salesperson and I had to remind her, "You know, a lot of people go into slumps. It's just part of being a salesperson. If I made every sale, I'd be eating bon bons on the beach in Aruba."

So I said to my sister, "It's nine o'clock in the morning." And I asked her, "What kind of realistic goal can we set for, let's say two o'clock this afternoon?" Maintaining that idea, I kept on asking her, "What do you want to hit? What number do you want to hit at two?"

And my sister responded, "Well I'm working on this one deal. I'd really like to hit fifteen to twenty-thousand dollars. If I can get this deal, I can hit it today." So I said to her, "Choose your attitude. That's all I can say. Have a great day!"

I can visually see her leaving my house that morning, and about four o'clock she called me and said, "I just sold fifteen-thousand dollars today!" I said, "Wow! Congratulations!"

It was: 1. Changing her attitude. 2. Setting herself a realistic goal.

She knew she couldn't do $100,000. She knew she was lagging behind, but she set herself a more realistic goal. My sister said she knew that was what helped her turn it around.

So think about it. You're going to get goals set for you at work. You're going to have people breathing down your neck so you can hit that goal. Everyone has to answer to somebody. And unless you're the owner of the company, you're going to have goals set for you. So personally change it up. Challenge yourself, but set realistic goals. Life's too short.

You don't want to end up having insomnia over things like this because it's been proven that a lack of sleep will shorten your life. It can cause all kinds of ailments, so be driven, but not neurotic. Remember, we're keeping it real—and a healthy sort of reality.

Once you're on your game, you can increase by another mini-goal amount, but always have several goals you can be working toward. My sister got back on her game, so you can too!

So when you get to work, set those goals. Reality is reality, but if you have those bite-sized goals, you can do what you set out to do and feel passionate about being successful!

Chapter 17: Let's Chat

Never lose sight of the fact that the most important yardstick of your success will be how you treat other people—your family, friends, and coworkers, and even strangers you meet along the way.—Barbara Bush

There are no strangers here; Only friends you haven't yet met. —William Butler Yeats

Good things happen when you meet strangers.—Yo-Yo Ma

The way to get started is to quit talking and begin doing.—Walt Disney

When the mind is thinking it is talking to itself.—Plato

When a [person] is talking to you, listen to what [they say] with [their] eyes.—Victor Hugo

It's weird how people who are the least close to me or who've never even met me purport to be experts on the real me; and then, sadly, there are those who could be in touch with me but prefer to gossip with strangers about me instead. —Vanna Bonta

The opposite of talking isn't listening.
The opposite of talking is waiting.
—Fran Lebowitz

This has been an interesting process in writing my first book, and it all started with my students running up to me after my training sessions, asking if they could buy my book—which I had yet to write. The point is, they felt comfortable approaching me after we'd gone through a training session, and they came up to chat. If they were hesitant before, they weren't anymore. And that's all that sales is all about.

It's about chatting with your customer who is already there to buy something. Your job is just to match them up with the right product. You know your product, so you're just chatting with them to see what the right product is and then selling them the value on that product.

Now we've all heard before that conversation is an art. Maybe you don't feel like you can wield a paintbrush, but that's not what you need to chat with a customer. You just need to be open to listening to them, then pointing them in the right direction.

That's why I teach an invaluable listening skills course. You're not there to just talk to yourself. If you were you might be in the wrong place! And thinking of your own agenda, instead of listening to the customer's signals, may get you off-track with the customer who would have been pointing you in the right direction.

You may have noticed I have more quotes in this chapter, but it was just too hard to leave any of them out. You might wonder why I have Walt Disney's as his seems to be about action, but that's just it. It's about actively listening to your customer, not just talking to hear yourself. You may miss what the real objection is or the qualifying answer that would point you in the right direction.

Fran Lebowitz's is the best as that addresses my pet peeve. You need to wait for the customer's answer versus trying to rush them through the process. You can't skip any of the process or your sales technique will falter and your numbers will start slipping.

Remember, you're not answering their questions with what you want them to buy. And you don't know them, so don't make assumptions. You're just chatting them up to find the right product. That doesn't mean that you can't tell them about the other products, but you're letting them do the talking.

So feel empowered and connect with your customers! It's all about communicating and listening to them. That equals trust, more sales and a bigger paycheck. Trust me on that!

And remember the first step in all of this. I realize it may take time to build your confidence. Step one is to eliminate the word "can't" from your vocabulary.

> *If you think you can do a thing or*
> *think you can't do a thing, you're*
> *right.—Henry Ford*

When you think you can't accomplish something for whatever reason it may be and don't even try, you'll never know if you *can* do something new. It's okay to step out of your comfort zone and try new things. You may even be surprised by what you can accomplish. I wasn't proficient with the computer at first, and now I'm almost an expert!

If you still say to yourself, "I don't have the confidence to ask for the sale," or "I'm afraid to ask for the sale," then you won't be successful as a salesperson. Think positively. Realize you're helping your customer make a decision. You're just communicating!

What we worry about too often is being pushy or too aggressive. That's not true at all. Customers are asking for your help because they want to make the right purchase. You're asking for the sale—after providing the right product based on their needs. That gives you permission to ask for the sale. So, stop saying I'm not a confident salesperson. Look in the mirror, smile and say "I got this!"

Now start communicating!

Afterward

This is a sales book that just had to be written. Linda Pike is a sales trainer. She is very successful at what she does, training others to be successful and passionate about their jobs in retail sales.

She has been in sales for thirty years and has been conducting retail sales training seminars across the country for twenty years. Linda has often had attendees coming up to her afterward asking for her book, so writing this has been a desire for several years. She is inspired and passionate about what she does.

Linda wrote this book with Deborah Littleton. She is a writer, actor, and director. She is also very involved and passionate about the arts and arts education. Deborah is a marketing and public relations specialist and has been writing freelance articles for ten years in addition to teaching acting, creative writing, and illustrating.

Linda met Deborah on a plane from Houston to Sacramento. Before taking off, the plane had been stuck on the tarmac for an hour, and Linda noticed that Deborah was writing magazine articles. They struck up a conversation about Linda's writing a sales training book. And the rest is history.

With Deborah's encouragement, Linda decided to commit to writing about her passion and experience. Deborah is always challenging Linda to rise to the occasion and the next level in her career as a writer and motivational speaker. They both hope you will do the same and start by reading this book. Take Linda's advice, please: Be passionate and driven to succeed! And just chat with your customer! After all, sales is really just about communication.

Notes

Notes

Notes

www.ingramcontent.com/pod-product-compliance
Lightning Source LLC
Chambersburg PA
CBHW070827180526
45168CB00002B/757